CONTENTS

INTRODUCTION

The Expectations Game is a staff development tool for principals who want to engage their staff in a discussion about high expectations. Research has identified high expectations on the part of teachers as being essential to the success of all students. However, just telling teachers to have high expectations does not often work. What you must do is thoughtfully discuss what high expectations look like and how they are "played out" in teachers' minds and work every day.

This game is designed to be conducted over several sessions throughout the school year, but it can be played in a shortened format. Directions are provided for the longer version, and options are included for the shorter version. In its optimum use, the game is conducted over 10 sessions during faculty meetings. Each session in this instance can be conducted in approximately thirty minutes (except for sessions 1 and 10, which are approximately one hour long).

The game format provides a fun, motivational way to address the topic of high expectations. Time is provided in each session for dialogue and reflection on this important topic.

PURPOSE

The purpose of the Expectations Game is to engage teachers in dialogue and reflection about the topic of high expectations for themselves and their students. An expected outcome is that through such dialogue and reflection, teachers will gain insight into their own belief systems and thereby be more open to changing attitudes that might be counterproductive to student success. Another possible outcome is that staff members will recognize in themselves the things they do that create a climate of high expectations in the school.

MATERIALS

In order to facilitate the playing of the Expectations Game, this book provides all directions, activities, and scenarios. In addition, portraits of the participants are provided.

GAME ESSENTIALS

Vocabulary

Participants: 10 teacher candidates; characters of game
Game players: staff members participating in staff development sessions
Immunity activity: activity conducted during sessions 2–9 in which one participant is declared immune from the elimination vote
Elimination vote: vote at the end of sessions 2–9 in which one participant is eliminated from the game
Scenario: story or description of participants' attitudes and beliefs about a given topic dealing with teacher expectations

The principal is the leader or facilitator of the game. Directions for the principal are included for each session.

Premise

The premise of the game is that school staff members have been charged with selecting one teacher to join the team in its efforts toward school improvement. There are 10 possible teachers, who are referred to as "participants." The principal has one caveat—the staff is to select the one person they believe will have high expectations for the students in the school. Each time the game is played, staff members are presented with a written scenario that provides more information about each of the participant's characteristics and belief systems. Time is provided for them to read the short scenario, reflect on what they have read, and make notes to themselves. The information provided in the scenario is intended to give all the game players more data on the participants so they can make their decision about who, in the end, is the most favorable teacher candidate and who they want to delete from the pool at each session (2–9). Beginning with session 2, an immunity activity is provided for the staff following the reading of the scenario. Each session has a different activity that is designed to produce one immune participant. Once the activity is completed and the immune participant named, the staff votes on who to eliminate from the pool of the participants for the remainder of the game. Before each new session, the eliminated participants are crossed off the scenario since once a participant is eliminated, the staff members (in terms of the scenarios, activities, and voting) can no longer consider this character. By session 10, there should be only two participants remaining. Then the winner is determined by a vote. An overview of the sessions follows:

OVERVIEW OF SESSIONS 1–10

Session 1 (Time: 1 Hour)

This is a somewhat longer session designed to acquaint the staff with the participants (the 10 people they will be evaluating).

Session 2 (Time: 30 Minutes)

This session includes a scenario about the 10 participants related to the topic of teacher standards and grading. Also included in this session is an activity based on the beliefs of teachers with high expectations.

Session 3 (Time: 30 Minutes)

Session 3 provides a scenario on the topic of discipline. The follow-up activity is a "word splash," which provides staff members an opportunity to reflect on the characteristics and belief systems of the participants.

Session 4 (Time: 30 Minutes)

Session 4 deals with relationships within a school community: student to student, teacher to student, and teacher to teacher. The activity is a game of *Jeopardy* that tests the faculty on what they have learned about the characters thus far.

Session 5 (Time: 30 Minutes)

The scenario in session 5 addresses instructional practices and student motivation. "You Be the Judge" is the activity in which participants are observed in a problem-solving session, role-played by volunteer staff members.

Session 6 (Time: 30 Minutes)

Session 6 looks at teacher expectations as told through lesson plans. The lessons are ranked on the basis of their strengths and weaknesses.

Session 7 (Time: 30 Minutes)

In this scenario, the participants are involved in a faculty meeting to develop a policy on retention and placement of students. A placemat activity follows in which staff members have a further opportunity to reflect on the suitability of each of the remaining participants.

Session 8 (Time: 30 Minutes)

Session 8 deals with monitoring and accountability, and the teachers' opinions of this topic. The immunity activity for the session is merely a physical challenge.

Session 9 (Time: 30 Minutes)

Scenario 9 uses a survey form to evaluate a staff development session. The forms are evaluated for honesty and possible implementation, and a name is drawn to determine immunity.

Session 10 (Time: 1 Hour)

The final scenario finds the participants at an end-of-year get-together in which they reflect on the past year, their summer plans, and so on. A vote will determine the final winner. A culminating activity that allows for reflection and discussion about expectations is provided.

OPTIONS FOR PLAYING THE GAME

1. Optimally, the Expectations Game is designed with 10 sessions, one for each month of the school year. If 10 sessions is not possible, it is the leader's responsibility to predetermine how many sessions are feasible and then (a) read all 10 session scenarios and choose those scenarios that most directly apply to the needs of his or her campus, (b) choose participants in equal numbers to the number of scenarios using the same criteria, and (c) set the calendar for the year.

2. Participants and game players can be set up in different ways, always remembering that dialogue and reflection are the goals of the game. Recommendations for different scenarios are suggested in the directions for each session. The immunity activity should be considered in determining how game players are best arranged for each session. Sessions may involve role playing, while others are best set up as cooperative group activities as well as discussion groups. At times, to achieve optimal staff participation, teams of six to eight members will take on the role of one of the participants. More than one team may assume the role of a single participant, depending on the number of faculty members and the number of participants remaining in the game during later sessions. During any session activity, these teams would discuss and agree on the participants' attitude, response, and/or reactions to the scenario.

3. In order to develop a true learning community, the facilitator of the game may choose to have game players read and discuss articles on the various issues raised during the game. A complete bibliography is included at the end to facilitate this approach to staff development. If this option is used, be sure to include time during each session for review and discussion of the reading.

SESSION 1

Session 1 provides an overview of the Expectations Game and introduces the staff to the 10 participants. It will take approximately 1 hour to complete this session.

DIRECTIONS

Plan and prepare for the introductory activity:

- Read the directions for session 1, steps 1–8
- Decide the best way to divide your staff into teams
- Arrange room for both pair sharing and teamwork
- Make copies of needed materials:

  - Participants/Characters list on pages 5–7
  - Meet the Candidate Worksheet—Handout
  - Scenario 1: Faculty Retreat
  - Session Summary Worksheet (figure 1.2 on page 8)

- Collect chart paper and blank paper for activities

Step 1

Begin by telling the staff: *During the year you will be playing the Expectations Game. The purpose of this game is to have us engage in dialogue and reflection about the topic of high expectations for all students. Through the game format, we will have a fun way to address this important topic.*

Step 2

Ask each staff member to: *Find a partner and brainstorm why high expectations for all students is such a critical aspect of any school's improvement efforts. (3 minutes) Have the pairs share their answers with the group as a whole. Write the answers on chart paper. Keep the chart paper posted throughout the year while the game is played.*

Step 3

Tell the staff the premise and goal of the game: *The premise of the game is that you [your staff] have been charged with selecting one teacher to join your team in its continuous efforts toward school improvement. There are 10 possible teachers [which we will call participants] in the game from which you will select one. The one caveat is that you are to select the one person whom you believe will have high expectations for all our students. Your goal will be to end the game with the most favorable participant in this regard.*

Step 4

Tell the staff how the game is played: *The game is played over 10 sessions. At the end of session 10, the winner, or the participant you most want to join our team, will be selected. In today's session, you will be introduced to each of the 10 participants in the pool of possible selectees. After today, in each session (2–9), you will learn more about the participants and at the end of each session eliminate one participant from the pool.*

In these sessions, you will (a) read a scenario that gives you further information about each participant, (b) participate in an activity at the end of which one of the participants will be immune from elimination in that session, and (c) vote for which of the remaining participants you think should be eliminated from the pool. Are there any questions?

Step 5

To introduce the participants, distribute copies of The Participants/ Characters list on pages 5–7 of this session, which provides both descriptions and drawings of each participant. Provide copies of the Meet the Candidate Worksheet to each person for his or her own reference.

Tell the staff: *As I introduce each teacher candidate, you may want to make brief notes on the session worksheet, which I will provide at the same time I give you this handout.*

Note: It is also suggested that each staff member be given a folder in which to keep all handouts. The Session Summary Worksheet (figure 1.2 on page 8) is to be kept by each staff member throughout the game. It is to be used as the staff member's "memory" from one session to the next and throughout the game.

Step 6

Activity: Meet the Candidate Worksheet

a. *On a plain sheet of paper, make three columns and 10 rows. In the first column, list the names of the 10 participants. In the remaining two columns, write two adjectives to describe each participant based on what you know about them now. (You may also hand out the "Meet the Candidate" worksheet to save time. An example of this worksheet is shown on the following page in figure 1.1, and the blank handout worksheet is provided at the end of this session.) Take 5 minutes to complete this task.*

b. After the staff members have completed this task, tell them: *Find a partner and share your list with him or her. See if your adjectives agree or if you have big differences. Discuss. Take 5 minutes to do this.*

Step 7

Next, have the staff members read Scenario 1: *Next, I will provide you with Scenario 1, which will further acquaint you with the participants.*

PARTICIPANTS	ADJECTIVE	ADJECTIVE
JONAH	organizer	mathematical

Figure 1.1.   Meet the Candidate Worksheet—Example.

As you will recall, I told you earlier that at each session you will be given a scenario that shows the participants in a particular setting and that gives you insight into their beliefs and characteristics. Scenario 1 is about goal setting. [Distribute Scenario 1.] Read the scenario to yourself in the next 5 minutes. Remember to take notes on your worksheet.

Once everyone has read the scenario, have staff members complete Activity 2: *Now that you have read Scenario 1, you know a little more about each participant. Go back to the list of adjectives you gave to describe each participant in Activity 1. Change any that you no longer feel are applicable or that need revision (5 minutes). Now go back to your partner to see if any of his or hers changed as well. Then ask yourselves which one(s) you think right now would be someone you would like to have on your team.*

Step 8

This ends session 1.

PARTICIPANTS/CHARACTERS

Jonah is a 25-year-old teacher with a master's degree in education. Although he is a novice teacher, he has already shown leadership by organizing a student math club and volunteering to participate on the school's parental involvement committee. The team leader/department head has commented to the principal that he always contributes in team planning sessions. Jonah often organizes Friday afternoon get-togethers at a local gathering place. The turnout by young single female teachers has been high because of his "leadership."

Abigail is 29 years old (again) with 12 years of teaching experience. Of high intellect, she is a very innovative, creative teacher. Although several teachers have indicated an interest in some of her ideas, Abigail "plays it close to the hip." She knows that she deserves credit for these creative ideas, and she is not anxious to share her glory. A quiet person, she spends most of her time "thinking creatively" in her room by herself. Needless to say, she has not joined Jonah's "team" after work on Fridays.

Paige is a 23-year-old first-year teacher. Paige came to this school enthusiastic and energetic about her new career. Reminiscent of a puppy dog, she has latched on to her team leader/department head, Carlotta, following her every word religiously. Paige does attend Jonah's team meetings with equal enthusiasm and energy.

Hans is a bilingual 32-year-old with two years of teaching experience. Hans is totally assured that he knows how to run a "tight ship." He is known for adamantly expressing his ideas privately and publicly. He is appalled by what he considers lax discipline in the school, and he is not about to "go down with the ship" if things don't improve. His booming voice and military style demeanor have often disrupted Jonah's Friday afternoon social hour.

Carlotta is 25 years old with four years of teaching experience. A team leader/department head, she openly and enthusiastically shares her expertise and enjoys her mentoring role. Underneath this "mothering, positive image," however, lurks a rather superior attitude. Carlotta would never mingle with the families living in the community. Rather, she envisions herself "more the type" to be highlighted on *Life Styles of the Rich and Famous*. One eye is always out looking for a higher-paying job or a benefactor.

Ramón is a bilingual 35-year-old with 10 years of experience. Ramón is on an upwardly bound career path. Administrators speak more highly of him than his peers. In constant motion (what with all his "professional climbing" activities), he hardly has time to "fire off" his weekly lesson plans. Often seen smiling and chatting with upper management, he has moved away from the Friday afternoon after-school "events" in order to be seen at "the right places."

Ernestine is 50 years old with 28 years of experience. Ernestine's bulletin boards are turning yellow around the edges. An advocate of "teacher lounge talk" with her close-knit group, Ernestine leads the team in her "deep understanding" of what's wrong with students today. Given that her car almost leads the afternoon bus out of the parking lot, she has not been seen at the Friday afternoon gathering or at any other professional gathering after hours.

Sue Lee is a bilingual 30-year-old with seven years of experience. Sue Lee "likes to be liked"—by the principal, in particular. She is also known for being agreeable on every subject, pro and con. She would never be caught stepping outside the bounds of school rules, and this has led to a rather inflexible attitude about change. This has caused Sue Lee some "grief," however, in that it is difficult to be an inflexible, hard-nosed "suck-up."

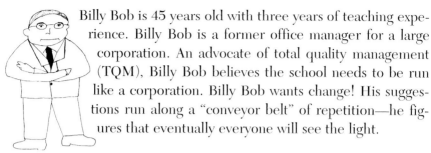

Billy Bob is 45 years old with three years of teaching experience. Billy Bob is a former office manager for a large corporation. An advocate of total quality management (TQM), Billy Bob believes the school needs to be run like a corporation. Billy Bob wants change! His suggestions run along a "conveyor belt" of repetition—he figures that eventually everyone will see the light.

Waylon is a 55-year-old with 30 years of experience. Waylon has no vision greater than the fishing hole that he will be regularly visiting in his retirement. Waylon is a controller of all, leader of none. Waylon loves a good joke and is a big talker. He is not where the action is. The boys in the school love his class, however. He makes the text interesting and fun.

Tracking of Participants: I = Immunity   E = Elimination

Abigail	I	E	Jonah	I		E
Billy Bob	I	E	Paige	I		E
Carlotta	I	E	Ramón	I		E
Ernestine	I	E	Sue Lee	I		E
Hans	I	E	Waylon	I		E

Notes:

Session 1	Session 2
Session 3	Session 4
Session 5	Session 6
Session 7	Session 8
Session 9	Session 10

Figure 1.2.   Session Summary Worksheet.

SCENARIO I: FACULTY RETREAT

Following is a scenario that will further acquaint you with the participants. The setting is as follows. It is before the school year has offi-
cially begun. The staff is at a retreat, and their charge is to
develop goals and objectives for the year. The principal has discussed
the performance of their students the previous year. The staff, working in teams, have been told to determine what instructional
area should be their priority in terms of improvement in the coming
year.

Carlotta immediately gets the team working on the task, assigning
Paige the role of recorder. Billy Bob says that they should use a prioriti-
zation matrix, a TQM tool, to determine their priority goals. Everyone
in the group ignores him and begins making comments on the data the
principal has just reviewed.

Carlotta interrupts their discussion to tell the group that she
doesn't believe the data paint the real picture of their student's performance this year. "We met most of our goals," she says. "Before
we go too far in this discussion, I want to remind you that if we set
our goals too high, we'll get penalized for not meeting them—so go
easy!"

Jonah responds, "Yeah, well if we set them too low, we won't challenge the kids—and I'm here to energize them!"

Waylon kicks in with, "I thought you were here to energize us, Jonah!"

Ernestine, ignoring Waylon, pipes in: "Well, it won't matter what we
do with some of these students—their parents don't care—what do they
expect from us, miracles!?"

Ramón interjects, "Miracles might well occur if we would just pay attention to research." He pulls out a research article showing how students have made high gains when teachers used techniques commonly
reserved for gifted/talented students. Several teachers scan the article,
and one asks Abigail if these were the techniques she used last year
when her students did so well.

Abigail, never one to talk much, responds, "No, I used my own techniques."

Ernestine says, "Well, we just need to get back to basics—the tried and true."

Sue Lee agrees with Ernestine but keeps her eye on the principal to see if she is on the right track.

Ramón and Jonah suggest that they all read Ramón's article since it relates to their high-need area.

Billy Bob snorts his disapproval. "We need to get a hold of the discipline here—first and foremost! That's our biggest problem!"

Hans agrees. "Put that down as our number one goal, Paige. Zero tolerance. Get them under control, they'll learn!"

Waylon responds, "Now Hans, you just need to kick back a little—make your classes interesting."

Paige says, "That's what I want to do. Make the classes interesting."

Sue Lee interrupts, "But we have to have rules, Paige!"

Carlotta suggests they get focused.

Several hours later, the staff have agreed on a set of prioritized goals and objectives.

On the way out the door, the participants have the following thoughts:

Carlotta: "Whew! This will be a hard year! I wonder if I will have time to work on my real estate license!"

Paige: "Thank heavens I have Carlotta here to help me implement these new initiatives!"

Billy Bob: "Man! That took a long time. It amazes me why they won't use my tools! We could have finished up hours ago!"

Hans: "Billy Bob and I got it right—discipline, discipline, discipline!"

Waylon: "I'm outta here! No sweat!"

Ernestine: "Heard it all before! We did this 10 years ago! Thank heavens I kept all my old plans!"

Abigail: "I'm going to go to the museum this weekend and get background information for a neat project that will fit right into our plan!"

Ramón: "I think I'll call Dr. X at the university and get some more information on their latest research study in reading."

Sue Lee: "I'll ask the principal if I can help her in any way—maybe update the school rules."

Jonah: "These kids are going to love this year! So am I! I wonder if some of the gang would like to discuss this more at our place!"

Meet the Candidate Worksheet—Handout

Participants	Adjective	Adjective
Jonah		
Abigail		
Paige		
Hans		
Carlotta		
Ramón		
Billy Bob		
Ernestine		
Sue Lee		
Waylon		

SESSION 2

Session 2 is related to the topic of teacher standards and grading. The scenario looks at the different attitudes and techniques used by the participants while grading student learning. The participants will be judged according to Belief Statements of Teachers with High Expectations. In this session, the first immunity activity is introduced and the first elimination vote conducted.

DIRECTIONS

Plan and prepare for session 2:

- Read the directions for session 2
- Decide the best way to divide your staff into teams
- Arrange room for teamwork
- Make copies of needed materials:
  - Scenario 2
  - Beliefs of Teachers with High Expectations (figure 2.1 at the end of this session)
- Decide on a voting method
- Remind teachers to bring folders and worksheets to session

Step 1

Begin session by reminding the staff of the purpose of the game: *The purpose of the game is to select the one participant you would most want to have join our staff in its school improvement efforts. The participant you select should be the one you believe has the highest expectations for all students.*

Step 2

To begin the session, set up the scenario with a short introduction: *Today's scenario will again give you more insight into the beliefs and attitudes of our 10 teacher candidates. Scenario 2 is related to teacher standards and grading. The scenario looks at the different attitudes and techniques used by the participants while grading student learning. After receiving grade distribution data at the end of the first grading period, which the principal does as a part of the school's monitoring system, Sue Lee receives an e-mail from the principal requesting a conference. I will now give you Scenario 2 for your reading, reflecting, and note taking. (10 minutes)*

Step 3

Immunity Activity: Belief Systems
Materials: Beliefs of Teachers with High Expectations (figure 2.1)
Directions:

a. Divide staff into teams, one for each participant. (If you have a large staff, you may need to have two teams for each character. Just don't let teams be so large that conversation is not possible.)
b. Assign one participant to each team.
c. Give each team a copy of figure 2.1, Beliefs of Teachers with High Expectations.
d. Give teams directions: *On the Beliefs sheet, mark each statement your participant believes. Tally the total of statements marked. (5–10 minutes)*

e. Have each team report total number of beliefs for their character. The participant with the highest number of beliefs is immune from elimination for session 2. In the case of a tie, name the tied participant with the most teaching experience immune.

Step 4

Declare the participant (based on the outcome of the activity) who will be immune from elimination in this session's vote.

Step 5

Take a vote on whom to delete from the pool of remaining participants. (Remember the voting does not include the participant who is immune.) Voting can be conducted in numerous ways. The principal decides on whether to have each staff member cast an anonymous vote and then tally, have teams reach consensus on who they would vote to eliminate and then tally team responses, or select another method of voting as appropriate.

Step 6

Be sure that sometime during the session or at the conclusion, game players have time to write their thoughts on the Session Summary Worksheet (see figure 1.2 in session 1). In reflecting on the different scenarios, the following ideas may be used to start discussion:

- What does this have to do with expectations?
- Who seems to be ignoring the problem?
- Who seems to be adding to the problem?
- Who sees the problem and is willing to tackle it?

- All students can learn regardless of difficult circumstances.

- The work I do with all students is important and meaningful.

- I can be successful with even the most difficult students.

- It is my responsibility to see that students learn.

- I examine my performance when students experience failure.

- I never admit defeat and strongly resist expressing a sense of futility.

- I pursue common goals with my students.

- I feel good about teaching and am enthusiastic about the students' progress.

- All students learn best when challenged with high expectations and encouraged to reach their maximum potential.

- A school is a total learning environment where everyone, including students, parents, and teachers, are continuously learning.

Figure 2.1.   Beliefs of Teachers with High Expectations.

SCENARIO 2: TEACHER TALK

After reviewing grade distribution data at the end of the first grading period, which the principal does as a part of the school's monitoring system, Sue Lee receives e-mail from the principal requesting a conference. The e-mail reads as follows:

> To: Sue Lee
> From: School Principal
> Subject: Grading Procedures
>
> Please see me regarding the high number of failing grades received by students in your classes.

Sue Lee, totally confused by this message because she has strictly followed the school's grading procedures, goes to Carlotta, the team leader, to ask for guidance in her response. "I gave the students exactly what their grades were. I taught the curriculum, and it isn't my fault they couldn't pass the tests."

Carlotta responded, "Maybe we better look at how you taught the material and how you assessed the learning so you will be prepared for your conference. What do you do for the students who are having trouble?"

Sue Lee: "I refer them to tutorials."

Carlotta: "We might ask around to see who had more success and what methods they used."

When asked for their thoughts, Sue Lee's fellow teachers responded as follows:

Abigail: "I just taught, but I can't remember how I did it. I just know I keep teaching until I'm sure they have it. I regroup for reteaching. Have you tried that?"

Paige: " I got the kids involved with a couple of cooperative learning activities. They seemed to really have fun and helped each other learn the material."

Billy Bob: "Don't ask me, I got the same e-mail."

Ernestine: "Oh, honey, it isn't your fault. The kids you have to teach don't want to learn, and until their parents step up and help motivate these kids, it doesn't matter what we do. Have you conferenced with all of the parents of the students that are failing? You need to see who is willing to help you."

Ramón: "You know our goal is to get all kids to learn. Maybe if you and I planned some lessons together, we could find the problem and correct it."

Hans: "I think your first problem is discipline. Are the students that are failing on task or disruptive? I think this is where you have to start. Maybe you ought to start sending some of those kids to the office so you can teach the good ones."

Jonah: "I sure would like to help, just let me know what I can do. For me, I monitor learning constantly and target those students having trouble for more assistance before I assess for a grade."

Waylon: "I can't really help you because my students really seem to like history. Maybe that is the key—they have to like the subject. Maybe you need to find something they like about what you teach."

SESSION 3

Session 3 deals with the hot topic of discipline. A "Word Splash" activity provides staff members with the opportunity to reflect on the characteristics and belief systems of the participants. This is the first session from which one of the participants has been eliminated.

DIRECTIONS

Plan and prepare for session 3:

- Read the directions for session 3
- Decide the best way to divide your staff into teams
- Arrange room for teamwork
- Mark the eliminated participant on the Scenario sheet with an X
- Make copies of the needed material: Scenario 3
- Collect large pieces of paper, markers, colored sticky notes, and other materials if wanted for the activity
- Decide on the voting method
- Remind teachers to bring folders and worksheets to the session

Note: Remember that there are only nine participants remaining.

Step 1

Remind the staff of the purpose of the game: *The purpose of the game is to select the one participant you would most want to have join our staff in its school improvement efforts. The participant you select should be the one you believe has the highest expectations for all students.*

Step 2

Spend a couple of minutes prior to the beginning of today's scenario and activity discussing who has been eliminated and why. This can be done in large groups, in small groups, or with partners.

Step 3

To begin the session, set up the scenario with a short introduction: *Today's scenario takes place in the teachers' lounge with the teachers views on the school's discipline problem described. Over the past few weeks, each of the participants has been observed sitting in the teachers' lounge chatting with colleagues. The big issue lately has been the discipline of the students. I will now give you Scenario 3 for your reading, reflecting, and note taking. (10 minutes)*

Step 4

Immunity Activity: Word Splash
Materials: Large pieces of white paper or newsprint and markers
Directions:

a. Divide the staff into groups of six to eight. (Nine groups would be ideal since there are nine participants remaining.)
b. Assign each group a different participant. Omit the name of any of the 10 participants who have been eliminated from the game.
c. Give teams directions: *You are to make a "splash" of words or pictures you would use to describe your participant based on what you know about the participant. You can either write words, draw pictures, or cut out pictures or words that portray this character. (10 minutes) When you are finished, post your splash on the wall.*

d. When all Word Splashes are posted around the room, tell the staff: *You will now move around the room to view the different splashes. You will then decide with your group which participant you think should receive immunity based on their expectations. Once you have reached consensus, you will attach a colored sticky note to the Splash of the participant you have chosen. The participant with the most sticky notes will receive immunity in today's elimination vote. (10 minutes) In the case of a tie, name the tied participant who is the oldest.*

Step 5

Declare the participant (based on the outcome of the activity) who will be immune from elimination in this session's vote.

Step 6

Take a vote on who to delete from the pool of remaining participants. (Remember the voting does not include the participant who is immune or any participant who has been previously eliminated from the game.) Voting can be conducted in numerous ways. The principal decides on whether to have each staff member cast an anonymous vote and then tally, have teams reach consensus on who they would vote to eliminate and then tally team responses, or select another method of voting as appropriate.

Step 7

Be sure that at some point during the session or at the conclusion, game players have time to write their thoughts on the Session Summary Worksheet (see figure 1.2 in session 1). In reflecting on the different scenarios, the following ideas may be used to start discussion:

- What does this have to do with expectations?
- Who seems to be ignoring the problem?
- Who seems to be adding to the problem?
- Who sees the problem and is willing to tackle it?

SCENARIO 3: TEACHERS' LOUNGE

Over the past few weeks, each of the participants has been observed sitting in the teachers' lounge chatting with colleagues. A big issue lately has been the discipline of the students.

Hans has been holding court on the virtues of an army-like discipline plan to "restore order to the school." His zero-tolerance policy also includes the implementation of a "time-out, boot camp–like" alternative center within the school. Hans believes that if the school gets tough on the students immediately, they will shape up and teachers can get back to teaching. He has already spotted a few "roughnecks" who would be perfect candidates to experience his plan firsthand.

Ramón has been studying the virtues of a discipline plan developed by a professor at the local university. The program has been researched in a few high-performing schools and seems to hold promise. Ramón has left several copies of the research articles in the teachers' lounge. He has been disappointed to find them being used as coffee cup "placemats" and as "notepads." One day, a particularly disgruntled teacher used one as a stress-relieving paper airplane. Despite this response, Ramón has scheduled a meeting with the principal to discuss this research. In addition, he has told everyone in the lounge that they can attend his presentation on this discipline plan at the next district staff development conference.

Waylon has been observing the "hot topic" teachers' lounge discussion on discipline with a wry smile. He is amused that so many teachers waste so much time gritching about student behavior. Through his years as a teacher, he has never written up a student for misbehavior. Heck! He keeps them busy working on hands-on, projects, uses humor a lot, and has even taken several of the incorrigibles fishing on occasion.

Paige has hardly made it to the teachers' lounge. She has been busy writing lesson plans, trying to organize her classes, and staying on top of things. When she hears that others are having discipline problems, she is relieved to know that she is not alone. However, she is finding that "getting tougher" on the students isn't working. All the teachers tell her to keep trying harder, but she can't help but feel sorry for a couple of the kids who give her the worst trouble. She brings this up in the lounge one day, and the teachers "boo her off the stage."

Carlotta, as team leader, is worrying about the impact that the children with discipline problems will have on the team's test scores. If it weren't for them, she tells the teachers in the lounge, they would have very high scores. She tells the group that perhaps they should "encourage those kids' parents to move to the next school district!" Even though she was just kidding, she has decided to call the parents in to tell each of them that their children are keeping the others from learning.

Billy Bob tells the teachers' lounge group one morning that the whole school needs to be reorganized before discipline can be improved. Someone suggests that perhaps Billy Bob can be named king, and then all will be well. Billy Bob ignores the remark and begins to lecture the others about systems change and the potential it brings to improving student learning. Billy Bob's point is that if students are learning, they are not misbehaving.

Ernestine has enjoyed her time in the teachers' lounge lately. She has found that many teachers are turning to her for advice. Ernestine's long tenure as a teacher gives them hope that she has some answers. Ernestine does, of course. She has always been a stern, no-nonsense type of disciplinarian who has no qualms in "taking off points" for bad behavior. Students are allowed no talking without raised hands, are assigned extra worksheets for disruptions, and may even get placed in a "special" corner of her room. Ernestine calls their parents immediately after each misbehavior. The other teachers are impressed by her control.

Sue Lee brought the school rules to the lounge one day and made remarks that some teachers were not holding students accountable for these rules. When told the rules don't cover every misbehavior, Sue Lee said that she would add anything they wanted to the rules. She is revising them for the principal.

Abigail never goes to the teachers' lounge. She is too busy working on her lessons. She has few to no discipline problems.

Jonah stops by the teachers' lounge regularly. He has been disturbed lately, however. It seems that everyone is so negative, complaining about discipline. He has tried to lighten up the mood by "acting out" some of the behaviors of their "favorite" students. He has made everyone laugh with these caricatures.

SESSION 4

Session 4 deals with relationships within the school community: student to student, teacher to student, and teacher to teacher. A game of *Jeopardy* will test the knowledge of the game players about the remaining participants.

DIRECTIONS

Plan and prepare for session 4:

- Read the directions for session 4
- Decide whether to use teams or individuals during the immunity activity
- Arrange the room for activity
- Mark the eliminated participants on the Scenario sheet with an X
- Make copies of needed material: Scenario 4
- Pick 10 statements or create your own to use in the immunity activity
- Decide on the voting method
- Remind teachers to bring folders and worksheets to the session

Note: Remember that there are only eight participants remaining.

Step 1

Remind the staff of the purpose of the game: *The purpose of the game is to select the one participant you would most want to have join our staff in its school improvement efforts. The participant you select should be the one you believe has the highest expectations for all students.*

Step 2

Spend a couple of minutes prior to the beginning of today's scenario and activity discussing who has been eliminated and why. This can be done in large groups, in small groups, or with partners.

Step 3

To begin the session, set up the scenario with a short introduction: *Today's scenario deals with relationships within the school community: student to student, teacher to student, and teacher to teacher. On this day, school begins with parents lined up in the office wanting to talk to the principal. The Robertsons are angry because their son says two other boys for no reason jumped him, and the parents want retribution. Mrs. Jackson is concerned because her daughter claims that her English teacher doesn't like her and grades her harder than the other students. The last group consists of Oljuwan and his parents, who accuse everyone, including students, teachers, and administrators, of prejudice. After listening to all the concerns expressed by the parents, the principal decides something needs to be done about all the anger expressed. The question in his mind is, "Do we have a problem with the way students are treated in our school?" He decides this is a good topic for the next site-based decision-making meeting, which is scheduled for the end of the week. The principal then puts out a memo announcing the topic for the meeting and invites any teachers with input to come to the meeting. This memo gets the grapevine going in the school. I will now give Scenario 4 for your reading, reflecting, and note taking. (10 minutes)*

Step 4

Activity: *Jeopardy* Game
Materials: 10 descriptor statements
Directions:

a. Divide game players into groups or select one player for each participant who will play the game.
b. Assign each group or player a different participant. Omit the name of any of the 10 participants who have been eliminated from the game.
c. Pick 10 statements for use in the game. Remember to use only statements involving those participants still remaining in the game.
d. Pick a scorekeeper. One point is given for each correct answer, and one is taken away for each incorrect answer.
e. Give game directions: *This activity will test to see how well we know the different participants. A descriptor will be given, and it is the game players' job to determine who is being described. One point is given for each correct answer, and one is taken away for each incorrect answer. The participant who gets the most correct answers is immune from the elimination during this session's voting. Since we are testing what has been learned so far, no cheat sheets are allowed.*

Descriptors	**Participants**
A fisherman	Waylon
"I'm better than you"	Carlotta
A loner	Abigail
Team player	Jonah
Studies effective teaching practices	Ramón
Longest tenured teacher	Waylon
Observant of others' behavior	Ernestine
Loudmouth	Hans
Lies about their age	Abigail
"Yes, Yes, Yes . . ."	Sue Lee
Loves organizational tools	Billy Bob
First-year teacher	Paige or Jonah

f. Give the statements out one at a time and have respondents give answers in question form when called on, thus the name *Jeopardy*.

Step 5

Declare the participant (based on the outcome of the activity) who will be immune from elimination in this session's vote. In the case of a tie, name the tied participant who is youngest immune.

Step 6

Take a vote on whom to delete from the pool of remaining participants. (Remember that the voting does not include the participant who is immune or any participant who has been previously eliminated from the game.) Voting can be conducted in numerous ways. The principal decides on whether to have each staff member cast an anonymous vote and then tally, have teams reach consensus on whom they would vote to eliminate and then tally team responses, or select another method of voting as appropriate.

Step 7

Be sure that sometime during the session or at the conclusion, game players have time to write their thoughts on the Session Summary Worksheet (see figure 1.2 in session 1). In reflecting on the different scenarios, the following ideas may be used to start discussion:

- What does this have to do with expectations?
- Who seems to be ignoring the problem?
- Who seems to be adding to the problem?
- Who sees the problem and is willing to tackle it?

SCENARIO 4: RESPECT

On this day, school begins with parents lined up in the office wanting to talk to the principal. The Robertsons are angry because their son says two other boys for no reason jumped him and the parents want retribution. Mrs. Jackson is concerned because her daughter claims that her English teacher doesn't like her and grades her harder than the other students. The last group consists of Oljuwan and his parents, who accuse everyone, including students, teachers, and administrators, of prejudice. After listening to all the concerns expressed by the parents, the principal decides something needs to be done about all the anger expressed. The question in his mind is, "Do we have a problem with the way students are treated in our school?" He decides this is a good topic for the next site-based decision-making meeting, which is scheduled for the end of the week. The principal then puts out a memo announcing the topic for the meeting and invites any teachers with input to come to the meeting. This memo gets the grapevine going in the school.

Waylon: "What do you suppose this is all about? Is he talking about how we treat the students or how the students treat each other?"

Abigail: "I don't see any problem. The kids in my classes work well together."

Sue Lee: "Oh this couldn't be about us. We do our job."

Ernestine: "I think we need to look at both issues. I see how different groups of students treat each other, but I also observe some teachers treating students without any respect."

Hans: "I give exactly what I receive!"

Ramón: "Our school is a minisociety and reflective of our larger community as a whole."

Billy Bob: "Yea! We're talking about solving the problems of the world. What can we do?"

Carlotta: "We look at our minisociety and at ourselves, attend the meeting, and make suggestions."

Paige: "What kinds of things do we suggest?"

Ernestine: "The one thing I know is that children copy what they see. We expect these kids to mix, mingle, and get along, but when we look at ourselves, do we do that? The teachers in this school for the most part form groups based on ethnicity and stay with their group. There is a definite division when you see teachers talking and visiting with each other. Is this the example we expect the students to follow?"

Jonah: "I try to get people to mix socially, but it is the same people who always show up for happy hour, and some ethnic groups are never represented."

Billy Bob: "What's wrong with people staying with their own kind?"

Ramón: "Perhaps we need to have an open dialogue about race and respect."

Carlotta: "Listening to all of you, I hear we need to set a better example for our students and do something about race relations among the staff. I suggest we go to the site-based decision-making meeting and suggest some open dialogue concerning both student relations and teacher–student relations."

SESSION 5

Session 5 addresses instructional practices and student motivation. "You Be the Judge" is an activity in which remaining participants are observed in a problem-solving session, role-played by volunteer staff members.

DIRECTIONS

Plan and prepare for session 5:

- Read the directions for session 5
- Choose individuals to portray participants in the immunity activity
- Set up the room for activity
- Mark the eliminated participants on the Scenario sheet with an X
- Make copies of needed materials:

  - Scenario 5
  - You Be the Judge scenario for seven participant representatives

- Decide on the voting method
- Remind teachers to bring folders and worksheets to the session

Note: Remember there are only seven participants remaining.

Step 1

Remind the staff of the purpose of the game: *The purpose of the game is to select the one participant you would most want to have join our staff in its school improvement efforts. The participant you select should be the one you believe has the highest expectations for all students.*

Step 2

Spend a couple of minutes prior to the beginning of today's scenario and activity discussing who has been eliminated and why. This can be done in large groups, in small groups, or with partners.

Step 3

To begin the session, set up the scenario with a short introduction: *Today's scenario takes place in the halls and classrooms of the school. Everyone in the school is busy trying to improve test scores. An audit team has visited the school recently to observe instruction and its impact on student motivation. I will now give you Scenario 5 for your reading, reflecting, and note taking. (10 minutes)*

Step 4

Activity: You Be the Judge
Materials: Copies of You Be the Judge scenarios for participant
  representatives
Directions:

a. Give the You Be the Judge scenario (on page 35) to chosen game players or to volunteers who are to represent the seven remaining participants.

b. Tell these game players: *You are to participate in a problem-solving session as if you were the participant you are assigned. You should play your role as closely as possible to what you would expect from your character based on what you have learned about him or her so far.*

c. Give staff directions: *Those of you not participating in the problem-solving session are to observe and then vote in groups of four for the participant who you think portrayed the highest expectations. The staff members representing each participant have been given a brief scenario. They are to be a member of a team asked to solve a particular problem. The situation is that one of the students in the school has been creating problems in the classroom of a new teacher. A bright student, Horatio, is totally unmotivated and refuses to participate in classroom discussions, complete his class work, or pay attention. Although he is bright, his reading skills are poor. He gets attention by making "smart remarks," acting tough, and bragging about how he is getting the best of the teacher. The class where most of his problems are is English/ language arts. The team's job is to give the teacher some ideas for addressing this problem.*

d. The participant with the most votes is immune from the voting this session. If there is a tie, pick a team (preferably one that did not vote for either of the participants who "tied") to decide between the two which participant should be immune from the voting.

Step 5

Declare the participant (based on the outcome of the activity) who will be immune from elimination in this session's vote.

Step 6

Take a vote on whom to delete from the pool of remaining participants. (Remember that the voting does not include the participant who is immune or any participant who has been previously eliminated from the game.) Voting can be conducted in numerous ways. The principal decides on whether to have each staff member cast an anonymous vote and then tally, have teams reach consensus on who they would vote to eliminate and then tally team responses, or select another method of voting as appropriate.

Step 7

Be sure that sometime during the session or at the conclusion, game players have time to write their thoughts on the Session Summary Worksheet (see figure 1.2 in session 1). In reflecting on the different scenarios, the following ideas may be used to start discussion:

- What does this have to do with expectations?
- Who seems to be ignoring the problem?
- Who seems to be adding to the problem?
- Who sees the problem and is willing to tackle it?

YOU BE THE JUDGE SCENARIO

The team of participants has been asked to come together to solve the following problem. One of the students in the school has been creating problems in the classroom of a new teacher. A bright student, Horatio, is totally unmotivated and refuses to participate in classroom discussions, complete his class work, or pay attention. Although he is bright, his reading skills are poor. He gets attention by making "smart remarks," acting tough, and bragging about how he is getting the best of the teacher. The class where most of his problems are is English/language arts. The team's job is to give the teacher some ideas for addressing this problem.

SCENARIO 5: INSTRUCTIONAL PRACTICES

Everyone in the school is busy trying to improve test scores. An audit team has visited the school recently to observe instruction.

Stopping outside Jonah's classroom, the audit team hears chanting and peeks inside. A group of students are at the front of the class doing a "rap" of mathematics facts and formulas. The other students are clapping and joining in from time to time. Jonah is doing a dance at the back of the room.

As the audit team moves down the hall, Han's class is "marching" to the library. Not a sound emerges from the students other than their feet making contact with the floor. An audit team member remarks that she is impressed by how quiet and orderly they are. Another member notes the students' somber facial expressions.

Abigail's door is closed, and there is a paper over the window obstructing the view inside. A team member enters anyway—she has some feelings of trepidation as she enters. As she enters, she is surprised to see the students in cooperative groups intently constructing architectural "marvels." There is a hum of energy emanating from the students. Abigail ignores the visitor and continues her consultation with one group that is solving a problem with their construction.

Sue Lee stops what she is doing and immediately goes over to greet the audit team member who has entered her classroom. She reminds the class to begin working on the worksheet she assigned them in case they were visited. Most of the class gets started, but a few earn dirty looks from Sue Lee, who is showing the visitor her detailed lesson plans and the rules for the class. One student raises his hand to say he doesn't know a word. Sue Lee tells him to ask a neighbor.

Waylon's class is having an active conversation about a historic battle between two countries. The audit team member steps to the back of the room to listen. It seems like everyone in the class has an opinion, and Waylon makes sure that everyone gets their say. Students respectfully listen to each others' opinions. Waylon suggests to the group that they form teams to study the issues involved and then create a different scenario to resolve the conflict other than a battle. The students quickly and efficiently get into groups with no explanation needed by Waylon. Not one student is observed to be off task.

Ernestine's class is quietly working on a practice test. Ernestine is at her desk grading papers as the auditor enters. She whispers to the auditor that she gives them practice tests regularly so that they will be prepared for the big state test in two months. She points out two students who are randomly staring into space and fiddling with their pencils. "These are two students who will never pass," she says to the auditor. They both were referred by her to special education, and she is awaiting the results. Noticing that one student has quit working, Ernestine reminds him that the scores last time were poor, so he had better be going back and checking his work.

Billy Bob's class is about to end as the auditor enters. Billy Bob is assigning homework. This is greeted by groans from several of the students. Billy Bob reminds them that in the corporate world there is no such thing as a 9-to-5 job if an employee wants to get ahead. Several students roll their eyes. The bell rings, and many race for the door. A few forget to write down the assignment.

Paige's class is divided into groups, and she is working with one group while the other three groups are busy with group projects. One group, however, is off task and discussing a new song by a favorite group. Paige finally notices and tells them to get back to work. The auditor asks one group what they are working on. It is an activity out of their textbook. They tell the auditor they are the gifted group and the teacher assigns them extra activities like this one so she has time to "catch up" the slow group.

Carlotta's class has a guest speaker, so she steps out of the room to talk to the auditor. Most of the group appears interested in the speaker, but two or three students are observed drawing, working on something else, or just staring into space. Carlotta tells the auditor that she invites people into her class for a "change of pace." "The students get bored hearing from me all the time," she says. She notes that this year's class is particularly unmotivated. "It seems like the work is too hard for some, too easy for others," she tells them. To counteract this, she has talked to her team about regrouping some of the children. She has told them she will take the low group and work on the basics.

Ramón's class is going on a field trip the next day. To prepare for the visit, he is having the students set goals for what they want to learn through their observations. Each student is developing questions he or she expects to learn answers to tomorrow. Some of the students have partnered up to write their questions, and Ramón has ensured that the one student with limited English proficiency has a buddy as well as the one student with a disability. The auditor observes that all the students have many questions that they are writing.

SESSION 6

Session 6 looks at teacher expectations as told through lesson plans. The lessons are ranked on the basis of their strengths and weaknesses.

DIRECTIONS

Plan and prepare for session 6:

- Read the directions for session 6
- Decide on the grouping format for the activity
- Set up the room for activity
- Mark the eliminated participants on the Lesson Plan sheets with an X
- Make copies of needed materials:

  - Lesson Plans (figure 6.1)
  - Lesson Plan Evaluation Worksheet (figure 6.2)

- Decide on the voting method
- Remind teachers to bring folders and worksheets to the session

Note: Remember there are only six participants remaining.

Step 1

Remind the staff of the purpose of the game: *The purpose of the game is to select the one participant you would most want to have join our staff in its school improvement efforts. The participant you select should be the one you believe has the highest expectations for all students.*

Spend a couple of minutes prior to the beginning of today's scenario and activity discussing who has been eliminated and why. This can be done in large groups, in small groups, or with partners.

Step 2

To begin the session, set up the scenario with a short introduction: *Today's scenario looks at teacher expectations as told through lesson plans. As the instructional leader of the school, the principal periodically and randomly collects lesson plans to monitor what is happening in the classrooms with curriculum and instruction. After reviewing the lesson plans in this collection, the principal determined that the curriculum was being covered but that the instruction varied greatly from classroom to classroom. I will now give you a set of lesson plans you will use for the immunity activity. (5 minutes)* See figure 6.1, at the end of this session, for the lesson plans.

Step 3

Immunity Activity: Lesson Plan Evaluation and Ranking
Materials: Scenario 6: Lesson Plan Evaluation
Directions:

a. Divide players into groups of two, three, or four.
b. Give directions: *Your role today will be to preview the lesson plans and evaluate them for strengths and weaknesses. I will provide you with a Lesson Plan Evaluation Worksheet. You will study the plans and fill in the sheet with their strengths and weaknesses. Then rank the plans from best to worst according to what they show about the teachers' expectations for their students. The teacher to receive the most number 1 rankings will be immune from today's elimination vote. (10–15 minutes)* See figure 6.2, at the end of this session, for the Lesson Plan Evaluation Worksheet.

c. With a show of hands, count the number of number 1 ratings for each participant. The participant with the most number 1 rankings wins. In the case of a tie, look at the second ranking, the third ranking, and so on until one of the tied participants takes the lead.

Step 4

Declare the participant (based on the outcome of the activity) who will be immune from elimination in this session's vote.

Step 5

Take a vote on whom to delete from the pool of remaining participants. (Remember that the voting does not include the participant who is immune or any participant who has been previously eliminated from the game.) Voting can be conducted in numerous ways. The principal decides on whether to have each staff member cast an anonymous vote and then tally, have teams reach consensus on who they would vote to eliminate and then tally team responses, or select another method of voting as appropriate.

Step 6

Be sure that sometime during the session or at the conclusion, game players have time to write their thoughts on the Session Summary Worksheet (see figure 1.2 in session 1). In reflecting on the different scenarios, the following ideas may be used to start discussion:

- What does this have to do with expectations?
- Who seems to be ignoring the problem?
- Who seems to be adding to the problem?
- Who sees the problem and is willing to tackle it?

NAME: Jonah

	Period 1	Period 2	Period 3
MON	Introduction: 1. What is ratio? Read p. 134 2. How do we figure ratio? Review multiplication and division facts with rock-n-roll song 3. When do we use ratio? Brainstorm 4. Pairs work, p. 135 Homework, worksheet 35	⟶	⟶
TUES	Check homework Complete explorer supply list in cooperative groups Homework: Write problems using data from supply list	⟶	⟶
WED	In cooperative groups, share homework, working problems together Redistribute student problems to individuals three times—grade Owners of problems check	⟶	⟶

NAME: Ramón

	Period 1	Period 2	Period 3
MON	What is exploration? Students complete chart as we brainstorm —what we observe —how we observe —tools of observation —samples to collect	⟶	⟶
TUES	Explain exploration project Divide into teams Assign exploration areas Go out to explore	⟶	⟶
WED	Teams study collections Write up observations Write conclusion	⟶	⟶

Figure 6.1.   Lesson Plans.

NAME: Waylon

	Period 1	Period 2	Period 3
MON	Brainstorm times in American history of exploration, including present day Give students opportunity to investigate periods in #1— choose which one they wish to study Divide into groups and formulate questions	#1 and #2: Same #3: Approve group makeup	Repeat period 2
TUES	Review sources for information Explain grading matrix Divide into groups; develop plan for study and presentation Get plan approval and begin work	#1 and #2: Same #3: Work with groups in formulation of their plans and assign specific tasks to specific members	Repeat period 2
WED	Cooperative group work period Rotate groups through library and computers	Same	Same

NAME: Abigail

	Period 1	Period 2	Period 3
MON	Introduce ratio, p. 134 Brainstorm situations when ratios are used in life Work p. 135: Pair check Homework: worksheet 135	Same Homework: Create a real-life ratio problem	Same Homework: worksheet 135
TUES	Check HW Create a real-life ratio problem in cooperative terms; check Redistribute problems for another team to solve Introduce Explorer Supply List Discuss how to figure for 70 men for 3 months.	Share homework in cooperative teams; choose one problem to pass to next team Work new problem Collect all problems In cooperative teams, revise Explorer Supply List for 70 men for 3 months	Repeat period 1
WED	Review Explorer Supply List In cooperative teams, revise supply list for 70 men for 3 months Grade teacher-made worksheets in test format	Teacher-made worksheets from student problems; grade Working in American history groups, develop supply list for period studying (figure in cost)	Repeat period 1

NAME: Hans

	Period 1	Period 2	Period 3
MON	Begin reading *Columbus Diary* Read chapter 1 Answer questions on worksheet Class discussion on chapter 1	Same	Same
TUES	Read chapters 2 and 3 Repeat	Same	Same
WED	Read chapters 4 and 5 Repeat	Same	Same

NAME: Carlotta

	Period 1	Period 2	Period 3
MON	Begin research project Look at Research Packet Explain expectations of project for A, B, C Handout due dates	⟶	⟶
TUES	Review note taking On note cards, take notes while reading in American history textbook Begin application to individual topics	Review note taking Group 1: Work on note taking from American history text Group 2: Work in pairs on text Group 3: Work in American history groups in development of cards for individual projects	List skills needed in note taking Practice as a class using History Ditto "Explorers" In pairs, make note cards from American history textbook
WED	Review outlining Using note cards from Tuesday, develop outline Continue note taking	Group 3: Continue using various resources Groups 1 and 2: Review note taking from Tuesday Begin working in American history groups (monitor closely)	Review note taking Check pair work Begin note taking on American history assignment

NAME: Billy Bob

	Period 1	Period 2	Period 3
MON	Introduce Exploration Period, pp. 33–45 Read Homework, p. 45	⟶	⟶
TUES	Assign explorer to each student Begin research	⟶	⟶
WED	↓	⟶	⟶

NAME: Ernestine

	Period 1	Period 2	Period 3
MON	Introduce Exploration Period by reviewing questions, p. 45 Read pp. 33–45 Answer questions, p. 45	Repeat	Repeat
TUES	Check questions Develop Exploration Timeline in cooperative groups	Repeat	Repeat
WED	Review questions, vocabulary Timeline using numbered heads together Quiz (grade)	Repeat	Repeat

NAME: Paige *(copy of Carlotta's)*

	Period 1	Period 2	Period 3
MON	Begin research project Look at Research Packet Explain expectations of project for A, B, C Handout due dates	⟶	⟶
TUES	Review note taking On note cards, take notes while reading in American history textbook Begin application to individual topics	Review note taking Group 1: Work on note taking from American history text Group 2: Work in pairs on text Group 3: Work in American history groups in development of cards for individual projects	List skills needed in note taking Practice as a class using History Ditto "Explorers" In pairs, make note cards from American history textbook
WED	Review outlining Using note cards from Tuesday, develop outline Continue note taking	Group 3: Continue using various resources Groups 1 and 2: Review note taking from Tuesday Begin working in American history groups (monitor closely)	Review note taking Check pair work Begin note taking on American history assignment

NAME: Sue Lee

	Period 1	Period 2	Period 3
MON	Pass out "Explorer" reading packet on multiple explorers through American history Review "Reading for Details" skill; mark questions on each; ditto that asks for detail Reading #1—answer questions	Pass out "Explorer" packet Write definitions needed to read ditto 1 (use context when possible) Check definitions; discuss which ones should have used context (underline clues) Repeat process for #2	Off
TUES	Check #1 (underline answers in text) Review "Main Idea" skill —Discuss main idea of each paragraph (In-Out) —What is main idea of whole selection? Reading #2—answer questions	Reading #1—answer 1 (details) Check answers (underline details) Discuss how to identify detail questions Reading #2—answer detail questions (underline) Check #2	↓
WED	Check #2 (underline details and stated main idea) Review "Drawing Conclusion" skill: What information do you use to reach conclusions? Find information #2 to support conclusions Reading #3—answer questions	Read ditto 3—Answer context and detail questions (underline answers) Check for grade Review "Main Idea"—stated and unstated Reread #1; write main idea of each paragraph and whole Check and discuss; repeat #2	↓

Participant Names	Strengths	Weaknesses

Figure 6.2.   Lesson Plan Evaluation Worksheet.

SESSION 7

Session 7 involves the participants in a faculty meeting to develop a policy on retention and placement of students. A placemat activity provides the game players with a further opportunity to reflect on the favorableness of each of the remaining participants.

DIRECTIONS

Plan and prepare for session 7:

- Read the directions for session 7
- Set up the room for groups of six
- Mark the eliminated participants on the Scenario sheet with an X
- Make copies of Scenario 7
- Collect large pieces of paper and markers for activity
- Draw placemats
- Decide on the voting method
- Remind teachers to bring folders and worksheets to the session

Note: Remember that there are only five participants remaining.

Step 1

Remind the staff of the purpose of the game: *The purpose of the game is to select the one participant you would most want to have join our staff in its school improvement efforts. The participant you select should be the one you believe has the highest expectations for all students.*

Step 2

Spend a couple of minutes prior to the beginning of today's scenario and activity discussing who has been eliminated and why. This can be done in large groups, in small groups, or with partners.

Step 3

To begin the session, set up the scenario with a short introduction: *Today's scenario takes place during a faculty meeting during which the participants are involved in developing a policy on retention and placement of students. There is a heated debate going on, and it appears that reaching consensus will be difficult. I will now give you Scenario 7 for your reading, reflecting, and note taking. (5–10 minutes)*

Step 4

Activity: Placemat
Materials: Poster board or large piece of white paper, one for each
   group, and markers or pens.
The board should look like what's shown in figure 7.1.
Directions:

a. Place game players in groups of six.
b. Give directions: *Place the placemat in the middle of the table within reach of each group member. Each member of the group, individually, is to pick three of the participants whom they have the most favorable opinion of at this point and write their names on the placemat stem closest to them. You will then share your answers. Your task is to then determine, as a group, which one you*

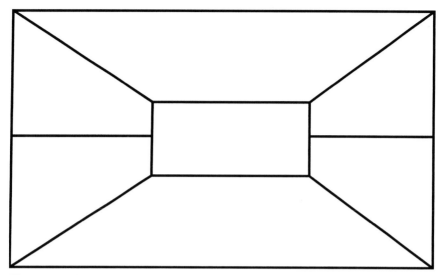

Figure 7.1. Placemat design.

> *believe is the most favorable choice. Each group will then share the name of their selectee. The one who is selected most often by the groups is immune from the voting at this session.*
c. In the case of a tie, name the tied participant who has been immune the least number of times.

Step 5

Declare the participant (based on the outcome of the activity) who will be immune from elimination in this session's vote.

Step 6

Take a vote on whom to delete from the pool of remaining participants. (Remember that the voting does not include the participant who is immune or any participant who has been previously eliminated from the game.) Voting can be conducted in numerous ways. The principal decides on whether to have each staff member cast an anonymous vote and then tally, have teams reach consensus on who they would vote to eliminate and then tally team responses, or select another method of voting as appropriate.

Step 7

Be sure that sometime during the session or at the conclusion, game players have time to write their thoughts on the Session Summary Worksheet (figure 1.2 in session 1). In reflecting on the different scenarios, the following ideas may be used to start discussion:

- What does this have to do with expectations?
- Who seems to be ignoring the problem?
- Who seems to be adding to the problem?
- Who sees the problem and is willing to tackle it?

SCENARIO 7: FACULTY MEETING

The school is in a faculty meeting in which they are developing a policy on retention and placement of students. There is a heated debate going on, and it appears that reaching consensus will be difficult.

Ramón has brought in several articles from the university that conclude that retention has a negative impact on students. He has distributed them to everyone and been given an opportunity to briefly discuss the conclusions from an overhead he developed. Many teachers talk through his discussion.

Sue Lee reminds the group that the school has a policy that they have been using for several years. She sees no reason to change something that has been working for them. When reminded about instances where it hasn't worked, she suggests that this resulted from a misreading of the policy, not from a problem with the policy itself.

Carlotta says that her team has already discussed this issue and has developed a proposal that the school might adopt. Three other team leaders say that their teams should have an opportunity to develop their own proposal first, and then the faculty can vote on the best one. Carlotta agrees but reminds them that "time is running out" and that her team has already identified 10 students who need to be retained.

Paige, being a recent university graduate, had already studied the latest research on retention. In her heart, she does not believe that students should be retained. However, several members of her team believe the opposite. Paige, being a rookie, does not feel confident enough in her position to take a hardline stand on this issue, so she stays quiet on the subject.

Billy Bob, noticing the differing philosophies, suggests that the faculty construct a decision-making tree to solve their differences. One teacher says, "Billy Bob, why don't you go climb a tree?" Billy Bob ignores him and says to the group, "As a point of focus, I think we all need to remember, that once these kids get into the work world, there are no 'free passes.' If we start from this perspective, perhaps we can reach agreement."

Hans tells the group that obviously some students will need to be retained. He would never consider sending someone forward who "can't make the grade." If we have a "tough policy," he tells them, "the students will know that we are serious, and so will the parents." Hans then says that, for pay, he will tutor students who are failing. He recommends a Saturday school with required attendance for these failures.

Abigail remarks that no one in her class is failing. She has set up her class in differentiated, flexible grouping patterns so that each student gets the instruction he or she needs. Abigail does not, however, share her plan with the group. She is unconcerned about the development of a school policy and considers it irrelevant. Her participation in the group decision making is minimal.

Waylon is anxious for the meeting to be over. He wants to stop by the sports store on his way home. He will vote with the majority just to get it over with. His philosophy is pretty much to pass students on if they work at making a passing grade. He also thinks it awful to keep kids two and three years behind. Usually they just drop out anyway if school is too tough.

Jonah suggests that everyone be given a break and, when they return, take an anonymous vote on whether to keep the old policy or develop a new one. If the vote is to develop a new one, he suggests that they have mini–task forces to develop proposed parts of the policy. One part would include a section on how to help failing students be successful prior to retention.

Ernestine believes that every parent of a failing student should be required to come in for a conference. At that conference, she believes they should sign a contract of what the parent will do to help the student. If the student fails anyway, then it's not the school's fault. She and her buddies volunteer to develop a sample contract during their off period tomorrow.

SESSION 8

Session 8 deals with monitoring and accountability and the teachers' opinions of this topic. The immunity activity is different in that it deals with a physical activity for the remaining four participants.

DIRECTIONS

Plan and prepare for session 8:

- Read the directions for session 8
- Select four game players to participate in the immunity activity
- Set up the room for the activity
- Mark the eliminated participants on the Scenario sheet with an X
- Get the chosen equipment for the activity
- Decide on the voting method
- Remind teachers to bring folders and worksheets to the session

Note: Remember that there are only four participants remaining.

Step 1

Remind the staff of the purpose of the game: *The purpose of the game is to select the one participant you would most want to have join our staff in its school improvement efforts. The participant you select should be the one you believe has the highest expectations for all students.*

Step 2

Spend a couple of minutes prior to the beginning of today's scenario and activity discussing who has been eliminated and why. This can be done in large groups, in small groups, or with partners.

Step 3

To begin the session, set up the scenario with a short introduction: *Today's scenario deals with monitoring and accountability. Concerned about something he has heard, the principal hands out an article from an educational periodical to the faculty for their reading and calls together a select group to discuss this issue. The principal begins the discussion by saying, "What gets checked or monitored gets done. What steps do we need to take to ensure what we want to happen in our school is what is actually happening?" Participants' views toward accountability are expressed in this scenario. The difference between monitoring and accountability is that monitoring is a daily activity that determines if what is expected to happen is what is actually happening. Monitoring shows progress, indicates areas where modifications to actions are needed, focuses attention, encourages future efforts, and holds persons accountable. Accountability is accepting responsibility. "Did we reach our expectations? Did we do what was expected?" In previous sessions, methods of monitoring have been discussed, such as grading, audit team visitation, and lesson plans. (5–10 minutes)*

As the leader or chosen faculty members read the following comments and opinions from scenario 8 (no names), the game players write down the name of the participant belonging to each comment or opinion based on what they know about each remaining participant. At this point, there are only four participants remaining. (Read only those comments of the remaining participants.) At the conclusion of the reading, let teachers discuss among themselves who they identified as saying what. Which opinion do they agree with?

Step 4

Immunity Activity: Fun!

The activity for this session is quick and fun. Teachers often monitor learning through games and fun activities. This is the premise for this particular activity.

Materials: Equipment for the chosen activity

Directions:

a. Choose one game player to play for each participant.
b. Choose from the following options or create one of your own:

  ○ Hula hoop the longest
  ○ Walk around the room the longest balancing a book on one's head
  ○ Locate a hidden object the quickest

c. Explain: *The activity for this session is quick and fun. Teachers often monitor learning through games and fun activities. Our remaining participants will see who can (fill in chosen activity). The last one standing will be immune from today's elimination vote.*

Step 5

Declare the participant (based on the outcome of the activity) who will be immune from elimination in this session's vote.

Step 6

Take a vote on whom to delete from the pool of remaining participants. (Remember that the voting does not include the participant who is immune or any participant who has been previously eliminated from the game.) Voting can be conducted in numerous ways. The principal decides on whether to have each staff member cast an anonymous vote and then tally, have teams reach consensus on who they would vote to eliminate and then tally team responses, or select another method of voting as appropriate.

Step 7

Be sure that sometime during the session or at the conclusion, game players have time to write their thoughts on the Session Summary Worksheet (see figure 1.2 in session 1). In reflecting on the different scenarios, the following ideas may be used to start discussion:

- What does this have to do with expectations?
- Who seems to be ignoring the problem?
- Who seems to be adding to the problem?
- Who sees the problem and is willing to tackle it?

SCENARIO 8: MONITORING AND ACCOUNTABILITY

The topic for today is monitoring and accountability. Monitoring is a daily activity that determines if what is expected to happen is what is actually happening. Monitoring shows progress, indicates areas where modifications to actions are needed, focuses attention, encourages future efforts, and holds persons accountable. Accountability is accepting responsibility. "Did we reach our expectations? Did we do what was expected?" In previous sessions, the following methods of monitoring have been discussed:

Session 2: Grading
Session 5: Audit team visitation
Session 6: Lesson plans

Accountability is expressed often by different participants as their attitudes and beliefs determine the degree to which they hold themselves accountable for student performance.

Concerned about something he has heard, the principal hands out an article from an educational periodical to the faculty for their reading and calls together a select group to discuss this issue. The principal begins the discussion by saying, "What gets checked or monitored gets done. What steps do we need to take to ensure that what we want to happen in our school is what is actually happening?"

Ramón: "Research says that if you want programs and training implemented, you have to be specific in your evaluation statements. For example, if we expect all teachers to use cooperative learning in their instruction, then we have to put in writing that 100 percent of the teachers will be observed using cooperative learning strategies during instruction."

Billy Bob: "In the business world, employees are held accountable, and if they don't perform to company standards, then they become ex-employees. Maybe we need to adopt this philosophy in our school."

Ernestine: "I think the answer is obvious. We need to hold the parents accountable. If the students aren't motivated to learn and the parents won't help, then how can monitoring my grades improve anything."

Sue Lee: "Well, I think what you want to happen is happening. We all work very hard, and although everything isn't perfect, we are trying. At least, I can speak for myself when I say I follow all the rules and do what you tell me. I don't know what else I can do!"

Hans: "You can monitor instruction all you want, but what you should be monitoring is the discipline. For example, how much class time is lost to discipline problems? What types of actions are taken by the administration when students are referred for disruptive behavior? What alternatives are available to teachers who have disruptive students in their classes? And I could go on and on!"

Waylon: "Look. I've been at this a long time. Sure I've seen a change in the students over the years, but I haven't seen much of a change in the schooling, and I don't expect to see any in the time I have remaining. I don't think you have to monitor me or the other teachers. Maybe the other teachers do need to do a better job of monitoring the kids."

Carlotta: "You know what I think. Maybe we should institute peer coaching. We have some outstanding teachers on this faculty, and we just need to do a better job of sharing what we know. I really enjoy mentoring new teachers and monitoring their progress. We as teachers are the key to this monitoring thing."

Abigail: "I don't mind being held accountable, but I really don't like other people in my class nosing around. It makes me nervous. If you want to check my grades and lesson plans—O.K. I'll even put together a portfolio of my work if you want, but please don't send other people into my room to observe or to check on me."

Jonah: "What is the problem and what is causing it? This is what we have to determine first. Are we teaching what we test? Do we have standards in place, and are our expectations high enough? I know I'm just a first-year teacher, but I learned while getting my master's that you don't try to fix something until you know what is causing the problem. Maybe we need to compare the state test against our written curriculum and then see if our standards match the curriculum and the curriculum matches the test. Then we can establish a process for monitoring the taught curriculum compared to the written curriculum."

Paige: "As a student, my work was always monitored, and I guess I just expected that when I became a teacher, I would do the monitoring. I don't guess I know of any other ways for you to monitor me than through observation and by checking my grades and lesson plans. Are there other ways? I guess it's just not a topic I've really had time to think about yet."

SESSION 9

Session 9 uses a survey form showing how each participant evaluated a staff development session dealing with higher-order thinking skills. The forms are evaluated for honesty and possible implementation.

DIRECTIONS

Plan and prepare for session 9:

- Read the directions for session 9
- Set up the room for the activity (This is an individual activity.)
- Make copies of Staff Development Survey Sheets (figure 9.1) for the three remaining participants
- Decide on the voting method
- Remind teachers to bring folders and worksheets to the session

Note: Remember that there are only three participants remaining.

Step 1

Remind the staff of the purpose of the game: *The purpose of the game is to select the one participant you would most want to have join our staff in its school improvement efforts. The participant you select should be the one you believe has the highest expectations for all students.*

Step 2

Spend a couple of minutes prior to the beginning of today's scenario and activity discussing who has been eliminated and why. This can be done in large groups, in small groups, or with partners.

Step 3

To begin the session, set up the scenario with a short introduction: *The teachers in the school have just participated in a full-day staff development session on the latest and greatest higher-order thinking skills program. As usual, there are mixed reactions to the training as reflected in their evaluations of the session. I will now give you the evaluation forms for our three remaining participants to read and study.*

Step 4

Activity: Staff Development Evaluation
Materials: Staff Development Survey Sheets (see figure 9.1, at the end of this session)
Directions:

a. Give directions: *Review the surveys of the remaining participants and determine which one is the most honest and most likely to implement the program in their classroom. Then write the name of the participant's survey you have chosen using the criteria explained on a piece of paper and drop in a hat.*
b. Draw one name from the hat. This person is immune from today's elimination vote.
c. Conduct the elimination vote. This will leave two names to carry forward to the final session.

Step 5

Declare the participant (based on the outcome of the activity) who will be immune from elimination in this session's vote.

Step 6

Take a vote on whom to delete from the pool of remaining partici-pants. (Remember that the voting does not include the participant who is immune or any participant who has been previously eliminated from the game.) Voting can be conducted in numerous ways. The principal decides on whether to have each staff member cast an anonymous vote and then tally, have teams reach consensus on who they would vote to eliminate and then tally team responses, or select another method of voting as appropriate.

Step 7

Be sure that sometime during the session or at the conclusion, game players have time to write their thoughts on the Session Summary Worksheet (see figure 1.2 in session 1). In reflecting on the different scenarios, the following ideas may be used to start discussion:

- What does this have to do with expectations?
- Who seems to be ignoring the problem?
- Who seems to be adding to the problem?
- Who sees the problem and is willing to tackle it?

TOPIC: Higher-Order Thinking Skills
DATE: April 26
PRESENTER: Joe and Evelyn Horowitz

RATE EACH CATEGORY ON A SCALE FROM 1–5, WITH 1 BEING THE
HIGHEST AND 5 BEING THE LOWEST:

PRESENTATION STYLE	☐1	2	3	4	5
PRESENTATION ORGANIZATION	☐1	2	3	4	5
HANDOUT	☐1	2	3	4	5
CONTENT	☐1	2	3	4	5
RELEVANCE TO MY TEACHING ASSIGNMENT	☐1	2	3	4	5

Should we continue this training?

Yes

What trainings should we pursue?

More of same

COMMENTS: I can't wait to use in my class. This is really exciting!

Sue Lee

TOPIC: Higher-Order Thinking Skills
DATE: April 26
PRESENTER: Joe and Evelyn Horowitz

RATE EACH CATEGORY ON A SCALE FROM 1–5, WITH 1 BEING THE
HIGHEST AND 5 BEING THE LOWEST:

PRESENTATION STYLE	1	2	☐3	4	5
PRESENTATION ORGANIZATION	1	2	☐3	4	5
HANDOUT	1	2	☐3	4	5
CONTENT	1	2	☐3	4	5
RELEVANCE TO MY TEACHING ASSIGNMENT	1	2	☐3	4	5

Should we continue this training?

No

What trainings should we pursue?

None

COMMENTS:

Waylon

Figure 9.1.   Staff Development Survey Sheets.

TOPIC: Higher-Order Thinking Skills
DATE: April 26
PRESENTER: Joe and Evelyn Horowitz

RATE EACH CATEGORY ON A SCALE FROM 1–5, WITH 1 BEING THE HIGHEST AND 5 BEING THE LOWEST:

PRESENTATION STYLE	1	[2]	3	4	5
PRESENTATION ORGANIZATION	1	[2]	3	4	5
HANDOUT	1	2	3	4	[5]
CONTENT	1	2	3	[4]	5
RELEVANCE TO MY TEACHING ASSIGNMENT	1	2	3	4	[5]

Should we continue this training?

No

What trainings should we pursue?

TQM, Dupont, Franklin Planner

COMMENTS:

Billy Bob

TOPIC: Higher-Order Thinking Skills
DATE: April 26
PRESENTER: Joe and Evelyn Horowitz

RATE EACH CATEGORY ON A SCALE FROM 1–5, WITH 1 BEING THE HIGHEST AND 5 BEING THE LOWEST:

PRESENTATION STYLE	1	[2]	3	4	5
PRESENTATION ORGANIZATION	1	[2]	3	4	5
HANDOUT	1	2	[3]	4	5
CONTENT	1	2	[3]	4	5
RELEVANCE TO MY TEACHING ASSIGNMENT	1	2	[3]	4	5

Should we continue this training?

?

What trainings should we pursue?

What does research say?

COMMENTS: I enjoyed the day and will use some of the ideas, but I'm not sure research would say this is where we should begin.

Ramón

TOPIC: Higher-Order Thinking Skills
DATE: April 26
PRESENTER: Joe and Evelyn Horowitz

RATE EACH CATEGORY ON A SCALE FROM 1–5, WITH 1 BEING THE HIGHEST AND 5 BEING THE LOWEST:

PRESENTATION STYLE	1	2	3	4	5
PRESENTATION ORGANIZATION	1	2	3	4	5
HANDOUT	1	2	3	4	5
CONTENT	1	2	3	4	5
RELEVANCE TO MY TEACHING ASSIGNMENT	1	2	3	4	5

Should we continue this training?

No

What trainings should we pursue?

Discipline management

COMMENTS: Our students can't think until they learn to behave!

Hans

TOPIC: Higher-Order Thinking Skills
DATE: April 26
PRESENTER: Joe and Evelyn Horowitz

RATE EACH CATEGORY ON A SCALE FROM 1–5, WITH 1 BEING THE HIGHEST AND 5 BEING THE LOWEST:

PRESENTATION STYLE	1	2	3	4	5
PRESENTATION ORGANIZATION	1	2	3	4	5
HANDOUT	1	2	3	4	5
CONTENT	1	2	3	4	5
RELEVANCE TO MY TEACHING ASSIGNMENT	1	2	3	4	5

Should we continue this training?

No

What trainings should we pursue?

COMMENTS: I learned new strategies. Thanks!

Abigail

TOPIC: Higher-Order Thinking Skills
DATE: April 26
PRESENTER: Joe and Evelyn Horowitz

RATE EACH CATEGORY ON A SCALE FROM 1–5, WITH 1 BEING THE
HIGHEST AND 5 BEING THE LOWEST:

PRESENTATION STYLE	1	[2]	3	4	5
PRESENTATION ORGANIZATION	1	[2]	3	4	5
HANDOUT	1	2	[3]	4	5
CONTENT	[1]	2	3	4	5
RELEVANCE TO MY TEACHING ASSIGNMENT	[1]	2	3	4	5

Should we continue this training?

Yes

What trainings should we pursue?

More of same

COMMENTS: I really liked the new Cooperative Learning activities.

Jonah

TOPIC: Higher-Order Thinking Skills
DATE: April 26
PRESENTER: Joe and Evelyn Horowitz

RATE EACH CATEGORY ON A SCALE FROM 1–5, WITH 1 BEING THE
HIGHEST AND 5 BEING THE LOWEST:

PRESENTATION STYLE	1	[2]	3	4	5
PRESENTATION ORGANIZATION	1	[2]	3	4	5
HANDOUT	1	[2]	3	4	5
CONTENT	1	[2]	3	4	5
RELEVANCE TO MY TEACHING ASSIGNMENT	1	[2]	3	4	5

Should we continue this training?

Yes

What trainings should we pursue?

I'm so new, I need everything.

COMMENTS:

Paige

TOPIC: Higher-Order Thinking Skills
DATE: April 26
PRESENTER: Joe and Evelyn Horowitz

RATE EACH CATEGORY ON A SCALE FROM 1–5, WITH 1 BEING THE HIGHEST AND 5 BEING THE LOWEST:

PRESENTATION STYLE	1	2	[3]	4	5
PRESENTATION ORGANIZATION	1	2	[3]	4	5
HANDOUT	1	2	3	[4]	5
CONTENT	1	2	3	[4]	5
RELEVANCE TO MY TEACHING ASSIGNMENT	1	2	[3]	4	5

Should we continue this training?

No

What trainings should we pursue?

How to get parents to care?

COMMENTS: Our students need the basics.

Ernestine

TOPIC: Higher-Order Thinking Skills
DATE: April 26
PRESENTER: Joe and Evelyn Horowitz

RATE EACH CATEGORY ON A SCALE FROM 1–5, WITH 1 BEING THE HIGHEST AND 5 BEING THE LOWEST:

PRESENTATION STYLE	1	[2]	3	4	5
PRESENTATION ORGANIZATION	1	[2]	3	4	5
HANDOUT	1	[2]	3	4	5
CONTENT	1	[2]	3	4	5
RELEVANCE TO MY TEACHING ASSIGNMENT	1	[2]	3	4	5

Should we continue this training?

?

What trainings should we pursue?

Let's have our teachers present their strengths

COMMENTS: Let's build from strengths within.

Carlotta

SESSION 10

Session 10 is the final session and will result in the remaining teacher with the highest expectations being chosen to join the school team. The final scenario finds the participants at an end-of-year get-together at which they reflect on the past year, their summer plans, and so on. A culminating activity that allows for reflection and discussion about expectations is provided.

DIRECTIONS

Plan and prepare for session 10:

- Read the directions for session 10
- Set up the room for discussion groups
- Mark the eliminated participants on the Scenario sheet with an X
- Make copies of needed material: Scenario 10
- Remind teachers to bring folders and worksheets to the session

Note: Remember that there are only two participants remaining.

Step 1

State the following: *Today is the final session of the Expectations Game. We have two participants remaining, and one will be our winner—the one whom we all agree would make a good team member and have high expectations for our students. Read Scenario 10 (5 minutes) and make notes on your worksheet as needed.* Note: Staff members need to read only the parts of the scenario related to the two remaining participants. After they have read the scenario, have them secretly vote for their winner.

Step 2

Conduct the closing activity: *Divide into groups of four to six. Brainstorm as many reasons as you can as to why the winning participant would make a good team member of our school team. What is it about this participant that will help our staff ensure that high expectations will be held for every student? Each team should have a leader, recorder, reporter, and timekeeper. Your group has 4 minutes for this activity. After the 4 minutes are up, have the reporter for each group report back to the group as a whole.*

Next, have each of the groups review the Participant Review handout (see figure 10.1 at the end of this session). *Our last activity will be to review what the authors of the game have to say about each of the participants and their pluses and minuses in terms of high expectations. Read "Participant Review," then discuss this information with your team members. Did the authors agree with you about why our winner was a good selection? Did we make a good selection? Why or why not? If not, who do you think would have made a better selection? Why or why not? (10 minutes)* Have each reporter share with the group as a whole.

SCENARIO 10: END-OF-YEAR REFLECTION

It is the end of the school year, and the staff are at an end-of year get-together. More relaxed than they have been in a while, the teachers openly express their views about students, school, and so on.

Jonah is the life of the party, patting everyone on the back, telling them what a great job they did this year. Jonah loves his class and thinks this year's was the best ever. Next year, it will be that year's group who are his favorites. Jonah believes his math club really helped math scores for the school and plans to expand it next year. He also thinks that if he can get some students with problems involved, it will motivate them toward improvement. In his mind, they can all be successful with some encouragement and attention. In the back of his mind, he thinks Paige would be a perfect "partner" in his math plan, but then again, there may be a new recruit—he asks Paige to dance.

Abigail stands by the jukebox thinking of how music could be incorporated in her lessons next year. She's not staying long tonight, but she would like to jump on a barstool and remind everyone of the honors her students achieved this year. Another teacher stops by and asks, "Abigail, how do you get such excellent performance out of your students?" As she picks up her purse to leave, Abigail says, "Through total dedication to them, that's how."

Carlotta thanks her team for another good year. She is smiling, knowing that she is signed up for a real estate course next week. After that, she's off to Europe for a couple of weeks. She has a seminar to teach on lesson planning in July. That will make her some extra bucks. Several of the teachers have asked her to have lunch with them over the summer. But, frankly, she's lost her desire to talk about school—"been there, done that."

Paige is telling the teachers that she will do a better job next year. She learned a lot from them this past year, and she thanks them for that. She does, however, secretly wish that some of them were not so traditional, putting "square-pegged" children into "round holes." She hopes she can get up enough confidence next year to "break out of the mold" more. She admonishes herself for letting two children falter behind when she could have done more. In fact, she's not sure she challenged any of them enough.

Sue Lee is still smarting over the challenges that were made to the school rules she developed this past year. She is still trying to convince the teachers that these rules are necessary to get the job done. She makes it a point to go over to the principal to volunteer for the job again next year. As the evening wears on, Sue Lee has agreed with just about everyone that their way of teaching, no matter how they teach, is the best way.

Billy Bob has cornered the principal and suggested that they attend a corporate training session on planning and decision making together this summer. Billy Bob's reflections are on the organization of the school this past year, and he has found it lacking. As for his own classes, Billy Bob figures he did a pretty good job with the students. Eighty percent were on grade level or above. "Not a bad return," he thinks to himself.

Hans is bragging to the others about how well-behaved his students were in his classes. Next year he may be even tougher! Although few students stopped by to tell him how much they enjoyed having him as a teacher, he doesn't mind. To him, that's not his job. His job is to make them learn, not to make them like him. And if they don't learn—well they had the opportunity!

Waylon is leaving tomorrow for a fishing trip. He hasn't turned in his retirement papers. In fact, he really liked some of the students he had this year. Two are joining him for a couple of days of fishing this summer. He has given a few others some of his favorite books to read. Maybe he'll retire the year after next.

Ernestine and her buddies are deploring again the lack of parental involvement in their school. Ernestine figures that most of her students will be goofing off all summer and lose what little their brains took in this year. "Oh well, that's somebody else's problem," she thinks to herself, "I'll get a new crew next year and try it again." Thank goodness she doesn't have to attend any workshops this summer, she tells the others.

Ramón is eagerly anticipating the completion of his administrative certification this summer. He would love to be principal of a lab school that implements research-based practices. He'll be teaching again next year, as it stands, but in the meantime his eye will be on administrative openings. He'll be glad to leave the classroom—he has bigger and better goals in his future.

Participant	Strengths	Weaknesses	Assessment of Players' Potential to Support High Expectations for Students
Jonah	• First-year teacher with a master's degree • Works at keeping fellow teachers' spirits up by organizing social activities • Shows leadership skills by volunteering for extra duties, such as organizing math club • Contributes to group sessions, showing he is a team player • Accepts responsibility for student learning • Instruction consists of unconventional teaching strategies that makes for a fun class, which is individualized with constant assessment of student learning	• Mimics students for a laugh with his peers • Playboy	Jonah sets high expectations for students and believes students learn best when challenged. He believes that not only the students but also he has a lot to learn in just his first year of teaching. He is enthusiastic about his work but is upwardly mobile and not likely to remain in the classroom for an extended period of time. He would be an asset for the short period of time he would be with you.
Abigail	• 29 years of teaching experience • Maintains classroom control through fun and challenging instruction • Ensures student success for all students through reteaching, flexible grouping to meet individual needs, and innovative and creative teaching techniques	• Not a team player; does not share her successful techniques with others • Does not participate in group problem solving	Abigail is an experienced teacher. Her expectations for students are high because her students are so successful in her class. Her strengths lie in her teaching, while her weaknesses focus around her isolationist attitude. She is concerned more with her own glory than with student success. She would have to make drastic changes in order to bring about schoolwide improvement.

(continued)

Figure 10.1. Participant Review.

Participant	Strengths	Weaknesses	High Expectations for Students
Paige	• Energetic and enthusiastic • Differentiates for ability groups • Open to suggestions from her peers	• Lacks self-confidence and ideas for change • As a first-year teacher, she is experiencing discipline problems	Paige is a beginning teacher who follows her leader and is open for suggestions on how to improve her performance. She could be easily molded. If the expectations are high among her peers, her expectations will be high.
Hans	• 2 years of teaching experience • Bilingual • Offers alternative solutions for his complaints	• A negative force in the school who constantly complains about the lack of discipline because he is experiencing difficulty in this area • Doesn't allow students to discuss their learning or anything else	Hans is a general who barks his orders and places all responsibility for learning on the students. His expectations are lacking, as is his respect for students. Hans would not be an asset.
Carlotta	• 4 years of teaching experience • Leader who mentors new teachers • Shares teaching ideas with others	• Superior attitude to the community • Teaches to the middle • Conducts large-group instruction rather than meeting individual needs • Believes it is the students' total responsibility for learning; if they don't do their jobs, then retain them	Carlotta is a leader in the school, but is not focused on her job. She is an experienced teacher who lowers her expectations rather than raises the level of instruction. She obviously wields a high level of influence in her present school, but one could question why this is the case.
Ernestine	• 30 years of experience • Has the "ear" of many teachers because of her years of experience and classroom control • Has potential for reducing ethnic divisions in the school • Monitors student progress • Believes in parent involvement	• Negative talk • Has stopped growing as a professional • Unwilling to change • Too many excuses • Classroom instruction does not model high expectations	Ernestine does not model high expectations. She will not likely change her strong opinions. She will keep her class under control, but she will not contribute to accelerated learning for all.

Billy Bob	• Knowledge of total quality management • Open to change • Knows a lot of management tools • Believes student discipline is important • Not a motivator • Not experienced or skillful in instruction • Very opinionated and not a strong team player	Billy Bob will probably not be welcomed by the team because he is too opinionated and tries to push only his agenda. His expectations for students are not known at this point. His knowledge of tools for planning is a plus, however.
Waylon	• 30 years of experience • Classes are motivating to students, especially males. He taps in to student interests and keeps them actively involved • Humor • Does not share his teaching strengths to build the overall school improvement and raise expectations for all students • Not a contributor to team discussions and planning	Waylon will model high expectations for students in his own classroom, but he will not bring this strength "to the table" to positively influence the overall expectations in the school. His eye will still be on retirement. If he is the selected participant, the school team will need to actively solicit his participation and contributions to the team efforts to raise expectations.
Sue Lee	• Bilingual • Agreeable • Will work to support the principal's efforts • Follows rules • Inflexible • Sometimes too rule-bound • Agreeable to a fault • Beliefs are not strong • High failure rate and refusal to assume responsibility for this fact • Classroom instruction does not model high expectations • Too willing to please rather than modeling a strong position of high expectations	Sue Lee does not have a strong belief system that reflects high expectations; however, if everyone in the school is modeling the belief that all children can learn, she will come on board. The concern would be whether such a belief system would become engrained in Sue Lee's behavior.
Ramón	• Bilingual • Administrators like him • Has good instructional skills, plans lessons to meet all students' needs, uses research-based practices • Sometimes focuses too much on upwardly mobile career path • Teachers don't always respond positively to him	Ramón has much to offer the team. He has high expectations for students. He is a good teacher. His knowledge of and interest in research-based practices is an asset.

ADDITIONAL RESOURCES

Administrators: Student Report Cards: Do They Earn an A or a "Needs Improvement"? (http://www.education-world.com/a_admin/admin068.html)

Building a Collective Vision, Developing a Shared Vision (http://www.ncrel.org/sdrs/areas/issues/educatrs/leadershp/le100.htm)

Collaboration in Schools Serving Students with Limited English Proficiency and Other Special Needs (http://www.ed.gov/data_base/ERIC_Digests/ed352847html)

Effective Educational Environments (http://www.ed.gov/data_base/ERIC_Digests/ed350674.html)

Expect the Best: How Your Teachers Can Help All Children Learn (The Executive Educator: EJ519766)

Expectation and Student Outcomes (http://www.nwrel.org)

Expectations for Students (http://www.ed.gov/data_base/ERIC_Digests/ed40960html)

Hiring the Right People. *The High School Magazine* 7, no. 2 (October 1999): 26–30.

If an Adolescent Begins to Fail in School, What Can Parents and Teachers Do? (http://www.ed.gov/data_base/ERIC_Digests/ed415001html)

Improving Black Student Achievement (http://www.nwrel.org/enorse/booklets/achieve/2.html)

Learning from the Best (http://ed.gov/pubs/1/Voices/learn.html)

Motivation and Middle School Students (http://www.ed.gov/data_base/ERIC_ Digests/ed421281html)

NCREL monograph: Raising Expectations to Improve Student Learning (http:// www.ncrel.org/skrs/areas/issues/educatrs/leadershp/le0bam.htm)

Schools as Learning Organizations: How Can the Work of Teachers Be Both Teaching and Learning? *NASSP Bulletin* 83, no. 604 (February 1999): 35–45.

Student Motivation to Learn (http://www.ed.gov/data_base/ERIC_Digests/ ed370200html)

ABOUT THE AUTHORS

Barbara Tucker has over 35 years of experience as a teacher, administrator, and district-level coordinator in the public school system. Since her retirement, Ms. Tucker's consulting work has focused on schoolwide improvement for high-poverty schools, resulting in student success.

Mary Jackson is director of special programs for the Fort Bend Independent School District (FBISD) in Sugar Land, Texas. With over 25 years of experience in public schools, Dr. Jackson has worked in school districts in the United States as well as abroad in U.S. military schools. Her career has focused upon quality instruction for students at-risk for failure.